Songs from the Back-in-the-Back

Marcia B. Loughran

A Publication of The Poetry Box®

Poems ©2021 Marcia B. Loughran
All rights reserved.

Editing, Book & Cover Design: Shawn Aveningo Sanders
Cover Photo Editing: Robert R. Sanders
Author Photo: Cam Sanders

No part of this book may be reproduced in any manner whatsoever without permission from the author, except in the case of brief quotations embodied in critical essays, reviews and articles.

ISBN: 978-1-948461-91-7
Printed in the United States of America.
Wholesale Distribution via Ingram.

Published by The Poetry Box®, October 2021
Portland, Oregon
ThePoetryBox.com

"So we beat on, boats against the current, borne back ceaselessly into the past."
> ~F. Scott Fitzgerald, *The Great Gatsby*

༄

"Once there was a rabbit—don't talk!! Once there was a rabbit—Don't TALK!! Once there was rabbit—DON'T TALK!!!"
> ~Cameron H. Sanders, Jr., age 6

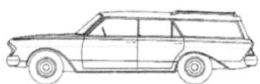

Author's Note:

Not everyone calls it the *back-in-the-back*. Some people call it the *back-back*, some the *way-back*. But if you grew up with long car rides and more than one sibling, you definitely got a turn to ride there: the rear of the car with the suitcases, lying on a thin layer of carpet, windows on three sides, and, if you didn't get carsick, the best view in the house.

Contents

i. poems for my father

Thirteenth Hole	9
Take Two	10
Look It Up!	11
Karma	12
Combing My Father's Hair	15
Baghdad, 1963	18

ii. family postcards

On the Road to the Thousand Islands	21
Estate Sale	22
Rowboats, Lake Mansfield, VT	23
7D Ranch, WY	24
First Away	25
Visiting	27
Send Me a Postcard	30
Miya's First Christmas	31
Taxis for Peace	33

...

Acknowledgments	37
Praise for *Songs from the Back-in-the-Back*	39
About the Author	41

i.
poems for my father

Thirteenth Hole

My father and I play golf
quietly. I walk, he rides,
we meet to look for lost balls,
whispering like librarians, conspirators,
murmuring encouragement
or sympathy. It's a hot day.
The gravel cart path
meanders like a river.
At the bend, a fox
sits upright, sentry.
In the ferns behind the tee box,
reddish-brown rustle:
second fox.
I hit first. Flashes of fur
dodge along the edge of the woods,
following the ball.
Halfway down the fairway,
the foxes form a gallery
and watch our second shots.
My father's errant drive
bounces on the verge beside them.
The closest fox
picks the ball up in his mouth,
trots back onto the fairway,
and drops it, improving the lie.
I hear my father laugh out loud.
Pleased, the foxes twirl
in and out of a sand trap,
leap, bounce onto the green,
and disappear.
Our next shots fly
straight, sharp, light.

Take Two

When I die I'm going to the movies. I'll sink back—
fake red velvet, the encompassing comfort of armrests.
My feet don't touch the floor, my father settles in beside me.
Names float upwards on the screen in curlicue fonts,
we call them out like old friends. Big-chested music
swells the dark. Our faces in the flickering light
are fish looking through water at the sun.
Classic movies: the only time my father stopped
telling stories. He let Ginger and Fred, Bogey and Betty
take center stage for a couple of black and white hours.
When the dame was got and the last song sung,
dance-tunes played us up the aisle. We stayed quiet,
stretching the feeling into the elevator,
resurfacing slowly, eyes adjusting to the pockmarked walls
of the parking garage. Starting the car, my father would launch
into a memory—the first time he saw the movie, maybe,
Scrap Metal Matinees on Saturday afternoons
at the Mount Lookout theater. During the war
they collected wagonfuls of cans to throw into a big truck
and get in for free, double feature, a Western
followed by Abbott and Costello. The whole ride home,
we get to be there too, 1940's Cincinnati,
a *Dolce Vita*, my father our Fellini.

Look It Up!

says my father—
we work at the kitchen table,
me on my homework,
him on a drink.
No shortcuts. He sends me
next door to the room
we call the *library*—
I don't know anyone
who has a *library*.
I stand under a yellow lamp,
turn yellow pages,
and dig,
scattering black letters,
skidding on dashes
and slippery italics.
Finally I carry
the dumb dictionary
into the kitchen, indignant—
It's not in here!
Or if I do find the word,
the definition muddles me more—
I don't speak lexicon—
till my father relents,
and reveals
origins, examples,
what the word means,
what it means
to be
that word.

Karma

*To the man who called my eighty-six year old father,
pretending to be his grandson,
claiming to be stranded at a wedding in New Jersey,
needing money to fly home.*

You nailed it.
How did you know
that particular grandson
has 'special needs,' is volatile, unpredictable,
this particular grandfather
overly generous,
a dutiful keeper of secrets?

The key to the scam:
*Don't tell my parents,
they'll kill me—*
leaving my father alone
to twist every turn
of the unlikely story
into logic and sense.

Did you wait until after
my mother died,
my sensible, skeptical, cheapskate mother,
who could've reminded my father
this California grandson
hates to fly, and doesn't know anyone
in New Jersey?

You knew my father was alone,
would keep his word, tell no one—

you've seen how far
a person will go
to save someone they love,
someone who in this case
was safe at home, oblivious.

Did you imagine
my father leaving his apartment
in the assisted-living facility
(aides, staff, helpers 24-7)
to drive to UPS
in a pandemic,
to send you money?

You did. You knew.
This is not your first time,
nor the last;
you do this for a living.
Well, know this.
Sometime soon
your life

will blow apart
in an enormous gust
of silence.
Everyone, everything
you love, hold dear, value, treasure,
get joy from, find pleasure in, live for—
in fact, the only reason you stick around
your sorry excuse of a wasted existence

[...]

will disappear. You'll be left
person-less, place-less, thing-less.
When somebody calls
pretending to be someone you love
you won't be able to fall for it—
you'll have nobody left to save.

Combing My Father's Hair

The last man in America to wear a coat and tie to fly,
my father's running late as usual, it's time to go—

he walks so slowly now and doesn't plan
for the extra time he needs to lose and find his cane,

he can't miss the plane, he's singing
a farewell tune for Freddy at the memorial.

More reunion than funeral, what's left of the gang
is getting together at Camargo,

the club in Cincinnati where they all grew up
swimming dancing drinking

upsetting their fathers' jalopies into the ditch
on the way home from deb parties.

Somehow in these stories a wedding party
always seems to come along to pull them out,

everyone gets home, it's the Fifties,
safe in their white ties and tails.

Now they're old,
he can't comb his hair without injury.

*I seem to be bleeding, would you mind
taking a look?* My father asks.

The white strands on his head
sprout reddish-purple—he has opened an old wound, a souvenir

of the latest encounter with a ceiling fan in a world built
for short people. Old skin so friable and surprising.

I wet a paper towel to clean him up—
don't get it on my shirt, he warns,

like it's my fault he's bleeding at the breakfast table,
my fault he's 86. I'm 52,

but to me he's no more than 40,
and I will always be ten.

I stand, he sits. I haven't seen the top of his head
since I was little, standing on his shoulders in the pool

breathless from the climb up his broad ladder-back,
feet slipping and sliding, pulled up by his outstretched arms.

I recognize the cowlick. Gingerly I dab
his dappled scalp with dish soap,

no time to find shampoo.
The suds curl his hair

into ivy tendrils over his ears—
same Dumbo ears as mine,

elegant elephant father,
circus elephant child.

The bleeding stopped, my father gets to his feet,
carefully folds the song he will sing

into his blazer pocket,
fixes his handkerchief square,

and gives me exact directions to the airport
I've driven to a thousand times.

Baghdad, 1963

Teahouses lined the dusty streets of the old river town.
On weekends, my parents left my sister, their first baby, home

asleep in the lap of Hannifa, the Kurdish cook, and drove the dunes
to camp, waking before dawn to walk the coolest hours of the day

among scattered bricks of ancient Sumerian villages,
looking for artifacts on the surface of the sand:

broken bits of pottery, figurines, beads, all that was left
of neatly irrigated fields and mud-brick villages

destroyed by Mongols from the North. As the sun rose
over Zagros Mountain, my parents prowled near Eridu,

entrance to the underworld. When Sumerians descended
to the watery kingdom, they did not go unarmed.

The dead were buried with maces, wooden staffs,
provisions for their journey. What will my parents bring

on their last walk? May they amble together,
two tall Americans, hats on, heads down. A willowy blonde

with legs up to here and the man she followed into the desert.
My father sings a ditty he wrote for cabaret night at the Alwiya,

my mother sighs and smokes a cigarette. They pocket amulets,
bicker over origins, gossip about the ones they leave behind.

ii.
family postcards

On the Road to the Thousand Islands

I remember humming in a nest of sleeping bags
in the back-of-the-back
of my grandparents' station wagon,
(this was 1976, seatbelts were for space travel)
when I was interrupted by a jolt,
and I was looking up at my sister's face
instead of at the back of her head.
I'd landed on the floor at her feet
behind the driver's seat: space travel.
There weren't enough ambulances,
so we had to share with the lady that hit us,
who was about to get married
and had run a stop sign. When she stepped
into the ambulance and saw three children,
staring, curious, she let out a wail
and cried all the way to the emergency room,
where my grandparents had already been taken
after smashing two solar explosions
into the windshield. They had to have stitches
in their faces. The scariest part
was the endless sobbing of the woman
as the ambulance rocked and swayed
and the siren sang. I didn't understand,
I didn't know the sting
of could-have-beens, the wounding power
of what-if. This was back
when everything
was concrete as a tiny island clinic,
regular as a quiet crossroads,
and time just something to hum to.

Estate Sale

How much could I get for the yellow porch swing?

> Let's see here—it's used—well-used. That's the thing.
> And it's big. Nowadays people don't have the space.
> Who has a front porch AND a patio?—what a place.

Try it! Three kids and a grandfather could all squeeze in—
not a splinter in four generations.

> There's a squeak. Quite a noise when it goes
> back and forth.
> I can't say if that might have effect on its worth.

Just the backswing—it's the sound of late afternoon—
the interlocked S's clink out their own tune—
of waiting for dinner, of Triscuits and cheese,
of kicking and sailing your own private breeze.

> You'll get fifty or sixty—it is the last day—
> it's a little bit heavy to carry away.
> Why not keep it? For you? For your kids?

I have none. I could maybe—but no. Go ahead, start the bids.

Rowboats, Lake Mansfield, VT

~For Liz and Sarah

We row backwards, heads cocked,
nudge between obstacles: boathouse walls,
shallows, rocks, our wide-bottomed boat unsinkable,

three seats long. The metal oarlocks
clunk and thud, correcting the long oars.
We wedge the narrow steeple bow into swampy bays,

dead trees our docks. Shallows
are for looking at the minnows change
their minds, change again, black bodies twitching

into angled arrows
on an underwater compass—
north, south, under the boat to avoid our dangling fingers.

Any child can row a boat,
anyone can go, grab a life-vest
and another kid, cousins are best

because they know
the longest songs.

7D Ranch, WY

It takes two days from anywhere to get to Sunlight Valley.
Play cowboy all week, wake up Sunday and you are
a Cowboy. Six again—Lincoln Log cabins,
red-checkered neckerchiefs, sitting on fences
waiting for supper. Fires light themselves, the horses
give you trouble only if you need it. Steep trails, slow trails,
one-eyed Uncle Bob will walk through wildflowers.
No matter where you come from, what dead-ass desk you sit at
day after day, the wrangler teaches you to lope, which is cowboy
for canter. Lean back, marvel at the sage
rollicking under Lefty's hooves,
and even if you grab the horn and lose your sunglasses,
you're riding the range, goddammit, God bless it,
as the sun sets on Heart Mountain, there's a place
in this country that feels, for a minute, like America.

First Away

My great-uncle, Gilbert Milligan Tucker, Jr.
grandson of a wealthy publisher,
(*Genesee Farmer, Country Gentleman*),
born in Albany, 1880, never moved away.
Died in Albany at 88.

Known (or unknown) family history:
Gilbert liked the ladies. Touring Europe
as a young man with his parents, Gilbert fell
for three Americans: Margaret Hays,
Olive Earnshaw and Lily Potter, headed home

on the Titanic. Gilbert wangled
himself a ticket, ditched his parents,
landing in cabin C53,
next to the girls in C54.
Gilbert eager to escort them,

fluffy bathrobes under lifejackets,
past the night porter's *Engine trouble*,
upstairs to the deck. All four listed
"among the saved,"[1] along with Margaret's
Pomeranian, in the log of Lifeboat 7:

> "Launched 12:45 AM,
> first away. Capacity 65.
> 28 on board: 25 first-class passengers, three crew—
> Mr. George A. Hogg, lookout in-charge,
> Archie Jewell, lookout, W. Weller, seaman."[2]

Capacity 65.
28 on board.

Margaret ended up marrying a doctor
from New Jersey. Back in Albany,
whenever Gilbert walked down State Street,
people crossed to the other side.
He could hear the mumbled whispers:

women and children first
women and children first

---

[1] *New York Times*, NY, NY, 4/16/1912.
[2] Hennessey, John M. Sadur, James E. *The Titanic Lifeboats Project*, 1998–2010.

Visiting

~in memory of Georgie

Obstructed view
from a hospital room
in midtown—

hard to get a bearing.
Find the river—
the river, always west.

The sun is out! attempts
my aunt from the bed;
it's cloudy and December.

So much construction,
she continues. She's right:
six cranes from here alone,

building buildings I have no
names for. I remember
teaching my nephew

New York City's skyline—
Chrysler, Citicorp, Empire State—
how not to get lost

coming out of the subway:
find the Twin Towers,
south, downtown—

not anymore.
The new World Trade, or whatever
they call it,

[…]

just another shiny building,
the kind they build in other cities
trying to be like us. My city

becoming a stranger.
I'm a Sunday tourist,
playing from memory.

Beyond my aunt's hospital window
a man stands at his window
talking on the phone.

He stretches, shirtless,
checks his watch,
turns away.

An Edward Hopper moment,
strangers glimpsed at unaware
and always a clock on the wall.

My aunt can tell time,
and gamely guesses
at the day.

It's been three weeks
since she was home,
and when my uncle sneaks

the family dog onto the ward,
it jumps into her crumpled lap
and licks her glasses off.

We're all crying a little bit
for the joy of it, the nurses too—
an unobstructed view.

Send Me a Postcard

Someone stole my identity to buy gas at a Quick'n'Go in Arizona. Some vagrant meth-lab escapee going to all that trouble for a tank of me. I imagine an irritable and overtired runaway-waitress character, Thelma or Louise, a faded good-time gal out of ideas in the middle of the desert. I go through my wallet to see what she got for her trouble. Student ID from 2013 I keep for the picture, several lapsed memberships of cultural institutions, a AAA card my parents still pay for, and a note from the blood bank that says I am a universal donor, O-negative. I haven't given blood since 9/11, when everybody in New York lined up, wanting to help, unable to help. Later we heard they got so much blood they had to throw it away. The needle hurt more than I remembered and I haven't been back. So now I guess I've donated my identity. I methodically cut up my two credit cards. Take it all, I think, buy yourself a carton of Kools, drive across the darkening desert, find a Mexican radio station and go. Don't bother looking for headlights in the rear-view, no one's coming. It's just you and the wobbly white stripes breaking up the blackness, under an invisible sky.

Miya's First Christmas

Born a few weeks ago, Miya sleeps in her car seat, sleeps through shrimp bisque and grilled cheese sandwiches, sleeps through dessert, sleeps through the presents Isabella bought us with her own money at the school Holiday Bazaar. Miya sleeps through Isabella's bedtime, Cormac saying good night, Tracey showing pictures she found in Olive's attic, pictures of all of us twenty years ago. Sleeps through Sean's mustache days, Valerie's one chubby moment, David's brown hair, Tracey's blond; sleeps. There's a picture of a shirtless David holding baby Seana, cigarette just out of sight of the camera, and here is Seana sitting on the floor, eighteen, home from her first semester, handing out University of Delaware ornaments. It's midnight, two days before Christmas; Miya sleeps. Valerie warns she'll cry if she wakes up, but we want her to wake up. We sit around her like we sat around Seana when she was a baby; Seana was the first baby; we watch the baby like people watch fire in a fireplace. Sean rocks the car seat back and forth with his foot; Seana moves in next to it; Miya's eyelids flicker, settle, flicker, slit open; she sees us; she's looking around; there's Seana, "Can I hold her?" and out of the car seat she comes, head heavy, floppy, a turtle, a sack of potatoes. Seana cradles her and tells Amanda, "She smells like baby!" Then it's Amanda's turn; she gets a smile; Miya's putting her tongue out, blinking, as Tracey kneels over Seana's shoulder making screeching noises. Not that long ago, Miya swam in a world of amniotic fluid, and she still moves like a fish, kicks her tailfeet as if to propel herself through water that has become air. Her fingers curl and

[. . .]

clutch; she will write and draw and make things out of dirt. We sit, lit by the Christmas tree, silent and inevitable. It's late but we don't want to leave, because this is the best story we know how to tell.

Taxis For Peace

I have a theory that as long as New York City cabbies drive the streets of Manhattan day and night without killing each other, we have a chance at world peace. Growing up, I knew a girl whose grandmother swore there would never be a nuclear apocalypse because of the New Jersey Turnpike. As long as we all keep driving on the New Jersey Turnpike without killing each other, we have a chance. I was explaining this theory to my Bulgarian taxi driver the other night after a couple of glasses of wine, and he seemed to agree with me, although maybe he was just being polite. His English was good but his accent was heavy. "Remind me where Bulgaria is?" I asked. "Eastern border with Russia, western border with Greece, north of Turkey, south of Siberia—" "*Siberia?*" I'm no geographer but that seems— "No, No, Serbia, Bulgaria is south of Serbia." I said sympathetically, "Do you have a dictator in Bulgaria?" He laughed. "No, we have democratic government. It was communist and now it is democratic government." I persisted—"Yes, but is it the same prime minister for years and years and years?" "No, no, we have elections; we have president; we have different prime ministers. Only problem is migrants; Bulgaria is gateway to Europe." The taxi driver knew how to get to my neighborhood in Queens, because he is my neighbor. He lives three subway stops from me. A lot of taxi drivers live or used to live in my neighborhood; they relax a little when I tell them my address, because they're driving us both home. They know to take the upper level of the 59th Street Bridge, turn right at the titty bar on 21st Street. We

[. . .]

talked about the neighborhood, about the difficulty parking Monday through Friday because of the stupid commuters from Long Island. He gave up his car, only the taxi now, his family rents a car when they go to Cape Cod—*Cape Cod?* Yes, Cape Cod; many Bulgarians live on Cape Cod—there is a well-established Bulgarian enclave on Nantucket. He loves Nantucket and much prefers it to Martha's Vineyard. He drives his family to Cape Cod every year, just like my family drove to Cape Cod every year my whole life, watching for troopers in Connecticut, no rest stops in Rhode Island, staring out the window at boring southern Mass. We argued about how long it takes from New York—he goes seventy the whole way and makes it in four hours. He arrived at my house in Queens in twenty minutes; I over-tipped and got out. I will never see him again, but next week, after a few glasses of wine, I will meet someone from somewhere else, someone who might want to talk after a long day making a buck in America, who might relax into the dark as we sail over the bridge, the Empire State blinking behind us. Someone who might glance sideways through the bulletproof glass and tell me a little bit about the world we both live in.

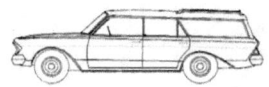

Acknowledgments

"Take Two" *Still Against War VII: Poems for Marie Ponsot*, 2017.

"Baghdad, 1963" *Ellipsis Literature and Art*, Volume 53, 2017.

"On the Road to the Thousand Islands" *Still Life with Weather*, December 2016.

"Estate Sale" *Still Against War V: Poems for Marie Ponsot*, 2015.

"Rowboats, Lake Mansfield, VT" *Still Against War V: Poems for Marie Ponsot*, 2015.

"Miya's First Christmas" *Pennsylvania English*, Volume 39.1, Spring/Autumn 2017.

"Taxis for Peace" *The Evansville Review*, Volume XXVII, 2017.

Thank You

Big brother Cam, my forever first reader. Little brother Nick for faithful copy-editing. Our father Cameron Sanders, Jr. for insisting on singing 1950's advertising jingles at the drop of a hat. The Irish, the English, and the Americans, who patiently sing along again and again: Mags, Brewster, Paula, Jess, Wendy, Olive, Tracey, Seana, Isabella, Helen, Julian, Nancy, Franny, Sarah F., David G., Corinne, Paul, Cusi. And David Loughran for sharing this long car ride and always bringing snacks.

Praise for Songs from the Back-in-the-Back

To say I'm a fan of Marcia B. Loughran's poetry is to put it mildly. *Songs From the Back-in-the-Back* is her third chapbook, and like the other two—*Still Life with Weather* and *"My Mother Never Died Before" and Other Poems*, the poems rock. Loughran's voice captures moments and scenes with a directness that brings the reader into the experience, whether you're in the "back-in-the-back" on a long family car ride, or you're taken back in time with her parents to Baghdad, 1963, when their lives together are just beginning. Loughran manages to write poetry that is funny, poignant, accessible—and inimitable.

—Nancy Jainchill, psychologist,
author of *Thai-Thai's Very Curly Tail*

I have known Marcia B. Loughran's father since the Saturday matinee movie in the suburbs was a Western followed by an Abbott and Costello comedy, and I have been "Uncle Mac" to her and her siblings all of their lives. I am, thus, not an unprejudiced reader of her poetry, but I admire her gentle but unblinking accounts of a family's foibles and inalterably deep affection. She reports her father's endless recollections of movies and of our misspent youth and also his endless loving loyalty, whether to a supposed grandchild in need or for a departed friend. Riding in the back-in-the back of a station wagon becomes a family tale akin to Mitt Romney's dog-on-the-roof. A weekend that Marcia spent caring for my hospitalized, dying wife becomes a reflection on urban displacement, Hopper-like visions in windows across an urban

[. . .]

void, and puppy-love. The same wry, loving, knowing perspective informs her rumination on extended family experiences. Marcia B. Loughran's penetrating truthfulness combines with her gentle and forgiving humor to create a healing and uplifting vision of her family and her world. We need more moments like these in our ruptured time.

—Milton McC. Gatch, author of *"Till the Break of Day": Philip Gatch and Some Descendants Through Three Centuries*

I don't read poetry because I often feel that the poet is selfishly trying to confuse me. I read Marcia B. Loughran's poetry. With her generous and accessible words and images, she touches those places in me that spark both memory and imagination. *Songs from the Back-in-the Back* is a gorgeous collection of Marcia's best family tidbits.

—Franny Forsman, Las Vegas lawyer and author

About the Author

Marcia B. Loughran received an MFA in Creative Writing from the Bennington Writing Seminars in 2013. Her work has appeared in *The New York Times*, *Verdad*, *Spoon River Poetry Review* and elsewhere. Marcia's two prize-winning chapbooks, *Still Life with Weather* and *"My Mother Never Died Before" and Other Poems* are available either at her website, through The Poetry Box or on a huge conglomerate website whose name shall remain nameless. Marcia reads her work in bars, bookstores and black-box theaters in New York City and the Catskills. She is a nurse practitioner and proud resident of Queens, NY.

<https://marciabloughran.com>

About The Poetry Box

The Poetry Box® is a boutique publishing company in Portland, Oregon, which provides a platform for both established and emerging poets to share their words with the world through beautiful printed books and chapbooks.

Feel free to visit the online bookstore (thePoetryBox.com), where you'll find more titles including:

My Mother Never Died Before... by Marcia B. Loughran

Nothing More to Lose by Carolyn Martin

World Gone Zoom by David Belmont

Notes from a Caregiver by Meg Lindsay

The Winter of J by Gary Percecepe

A Shape of Sky by Cathy Cain

The Very Rich Hours by Gregory Loselle

Shadow Man by Margaret Chula

The Widow at the Piano by Sue Fagadle Lick

Sophia & Mister Walter Whitman by Penelope Scambly Schott

Building a Woman by Deborah Meltvedt

The Kingdom of Birds by Joan Colby

and more . . .

www.ingramcontent.com/pod-product-compliance
Lightning Source LLC
LaVergne TN
LVHW090040080526
838202LV00046B/3898